Fallout

Fallout

Poems by Frederick Feirstein

Word Press

Published by Word Press
P.O. Box 541106
Cincinnati, OH 45254-1106

ISBN: 9781934999097
LCCN: 2008927498

Poetry Editor: Kevin Walzer
Business Editor: Lori Jareo

Visit us on the web at
www.word-press.com

Acknowledgments

Special thanks to Steven Assael for his graciousness in letting me use his painting *Homeward Bound* for the cover.

American Arts Quarterly: "The Frick," "Resonance"

Edge City Review: All of the lyric sequence "The Unholy Dark"

Ontario Review: "Father and Son"

Partisan Review: "In the Restaurant," "For My Father," "Half The Office," selections from "Dark Carnival"

Afterword which appeared in its shorter form in *Partisan Review* and in its longer form in *NAAP News*.

Pivot: All of the dramatic monologue "Dark Carnival," "What Happened," "Separation," "Mock Epic," "Home Movies," "Parents"

Poetry: "Immortality," "Spring Music"

Quarterly Review of Literature: "To My Younger Self," "The Pond"

Story Line Press: "Twentieth Century"

For Linda, as always

"... No one really knows what era he is living in. That is why we did not know in the early 1910's that we were living on the eve of World War I and the October Revolution."

Anna Akhmatova
My Half Century

"Don't read the newspapers"

Aldous Huxley
Time Must Have A Stop

Contents

1. 20th Century: A Sequence

What Happened

What happened to Mozart who sang like a bird
More golden than Yeats' imagination wrought,
Where is Shakespeare's passionate thought,
Does his ghost pace on Hamlet's stage?
And what of Dante who consigned to Hell
His former friends who did not treat him well?
Where is Sophocles whose simple myth
Became the basis of psychoanalysis.
And Freud who smoked his mouth to death,
What happened to him, to his depth
Of soul—is it lying like a clay shard
In an earthen hole, and poor Dylan Thomas
Who ranted "Death shall have no dominion,"
Knowing he lied, or the Brothers Grimm,
What became of them, dust in sunlight
Turned like a clock—watch it long enough
And you'll go mad, or Paganini
Whose fingers danced and women swooned,
Or Gower, or Chaucer who made
Such exquisite mixes of English and French
The birds that *slepen al with open eye*
Would weep to hear the Earth took him?
What happened to Donne who would have us listen
To sermons about our limitations,
And Boccacio, a name to stuff in your mouth
As a squirrel stuffs nuts when fall leaves redden?
What of Herbert with his convictions of heaven
And Apollinaire, that fantastic name,

Verlaine, Villon, Baudelaire, names
That once strode Paris, and Renoir, Cezanne?
What happened to Picasso, where did he go,
And Marc Chagall who would live forever,
And Michelangelo upside down,
Painting all night like a motley clown,
And Jane Austen, so precise about the minutiae
Of interactions, where is her flesh
With its intricate cells,
And Emily Dickinson who lived alone
As if time never happened.
What happened to Einstein,
His brain in a jar,
And Galileo, Copernicus, Blake?
Put them together and what do you make
Of these disappeared, where did they go?
We know but we are too timid to say,
Of Whitman who whistled his own way,
Hands in his pockets, ready to loaf,
Or Frost that dark and folksy man,
Beckett waiting in a garbage can.
All these geniuses and little you
With a pen in your hand, a non-believing Jew,
What of your life, where did it go?
It passed in an instant. Oh.

To My Younger Self

The past is like a library after dark
Where we sit on the steps trading stories
With characters we imagined ourselves to be.
Neighbors in clothing from our childhood stroll by,
Unmolested, nodding at us, benevolently.
One with your father's face tips his fedora.
You lower your face in shame. I look back.
Someone is sitting at a long table,
Reading in the moonlight. I must look startled.
He holds a forefinger to his lips,
As if it is a candle for the dead.
You tap me on the shoulder and I turn back.
The street is dangerously empty,
Except for the newsstand lit yellow
Where your mother in a blue nightgown
Showing beneath her coat buys *The Times,*
A pack of *Kools* and, eyeing us, lights one.
You race to her, turn a corner. Goodbye.
I'm frightened as if I'm a foreigner
In a city under siege. Yet I know
It is still mid-century. Underground
Are only subways carrying boisterous
Party-goers or somber family men
Working the night shift or harmless bookies
Respectful of the No Smoking signs.
I walk to where the newsstand, shut,
Advertises brand names I'd forgotten.
I shove my hands in my pockets and whistle

A song we danced to when we were young.
I walk on for blocks, until I smell
Smoke from the burning borough of the Bronx.

Twentieth Century

A winter evening under a John Sloan El.
Fedoras tilt in unison against the wind.
The pink neon lights of a Polish bar
Invite Grandpa in, while my son
Does pushups on the rug, and I chin
In my mother's kitchen, and my uncle
Argues he could beat Willie Pep
If Grandpa would let him turn pro. I burn
In his disappointment, forty years ago.
Now Grandpa comes brawling into the street
And, arm-weary, staggers home on schnapps
And sits me down to watch Sugar Ray dance
Till he turns into *Counting Crows,* and my son
In my uncle's pecks flexes in the window
Where stenos in thin coats huddle against the snow.
One of them my mother, seeing my unborn face
In a taxi, hails it and rushes home.

Separation

I ran out of the house
The world said Boo
I ran back to the house
My mother said I
I ran out of the house
The world said Die
I ran back to the house
My mother said Why
I ran out of the house
The world said Who
I ran back to the house
My mother said Lie
I ran out of the house
The world said Dread
I ran back to the house
My mother was dead.

Mock Epic

From darkness, where every hero goes
To find he's smaller than he had imagined,
I write a devil-may-care duet,
A lullaby for Bosch or Kurosawa.

Survivor guilt or curiosity
Drew me here like a seductive mother
Or the long deep notes from a sea god's shell,
From the primal scene, or from Sartre's hell.

I might have dramatized this when young and strong,
Made it a crisis in an epic poem.
But I'm too tired now to make this long.
Besides, all epics only take us home.

Home Movies

"Come home, come home," the failure family said,
"Where everyone is ailing or depressed.
We have washed your food, we have made your bed.
Come into the darkness and get undressed."

Have you ever watched an animal brought down
Step by tired step, traumatized and dazed?
I used to tap dance through my all-night town
Like Fred Astaire, debonair and unfazed

By the Depression that brought others low,
Squabbling around our wooden kitchen table.
I danced on my imagination's marble, slow,
While on the set Cain was murdering Abel.

"Come home," said Envy with its grin and wink,
"You are no different from the rest of us."
"Oh no, I feel so passionate and think,
Therefore I am." "Damn," they said, "don't cuss."

And kept on muttering hypnotically
How my strength was self-made and, therefore, weak,
Until they robbed me of my energy,
Until I joined them dancing cheek to cheek.

"I'm home, I've failed, I'm sick, depressed.
I'm nothing but a creature of your time,
Fleeing pogroms, a little Russian Jew,
A Chaplin shrugging, 'Living is a crime?'"

In our central myth, Dorothy tries to strive
Toward selfhood in a country green as money,
But learns she's merely dreaming to survive,
Tricked by the Wizard, just her Aunt Bee's "Honey."

"Darn if it isn't true," says Fred Astaire,
"There's no place like home, there's no place like home."
He's watching Judy Garland climb a stair
Made of marble, slick as a cemetery stone.

When small I thought my family film stars too,
Not as they were, I came to realize—as I dreamed.
My family were assimilated Jews,
Who dropped dead when their own ghosts schemed,

"Come home," like cozy families everywhere,
Hiding from cyclones in the gentile West,
Cossacks of wind that fractured Fred Astaire
And Judy Garland who came home to rest.

Father and Son

Finally I've learned forgiveness at this age,
For your mistakes that crippled me,
Which I've repeated. I have seen far worse.
You made them out of ignorance, not choice.

The rage I had, the wisdom that I lacked
Amaze me now, as if a page
That I was reading suddenly caught fire
And images of you tumbled from the smoke,
Words you mumbled when you were very tired,

Dying, your hand in mine, that long last night,
Both knowing you had lost all breath to fight.
"It's late," you said, "I don't want you to go.
But you have to leave me." So I sighed

And, like a child in winter, buttoned up my coat.
"I love you," we said simultaneously.
"Kiss your son for me," who then was four months old.
The next day you were found unsaveable and cold.

So if I try to save you on this page
And if you try to save me from your realm,
Eons away, distances so vast
It seems a microscopic stage our past

Of father and son struggling through myth
Which we enacted witlessly and sick,
Dumb, irreconcilable, compelled
To make this seeming paradise a hell

In which we sleptwalked like the shade you are,
The shadow of a man I hoped to be.
Why were we burdened, little you and me
Or, as you often said, "How can this be?"

Myths

Groping for consolation in The Final Stage
So we'll seem less crazy, for our childrens' sake,
We make our re-enactments *Tragedies*
Where we're heroic, though we know we're fake.

Or, atheists start singing of The Soul
Like Yeats, that loony we'd have ridiculed
When younger, braver, realer. Who'd believe
We'd harmonize in his strange singing school?

But, better, there's real comedy to tell
If we can find the insight and the will
To tease ourselves into those tiny hells
Where we, chronically children, all fall ill.

When he was lucid, Jung described the scenes
Where we're compelled to re-enact dark myths
That we can glimpse in fairytales and dreams,
As when he dreamed himself Christ The Fish.

Freud found his myth in self-analysis
Where Orpheus, né Oedipus, he led
Us lost boys, naked, to our soul's abyss
—To see in flashbacks what we missed in bed.

So ask yourselves, what myth became your Fate,
What traumas drew you in to play what part,
What self-deceptions, and what hypnoid states
Determined what exactly broke your heart?

Parents

Night after night, as Age walks through my rooms,
Like a clown waddling on stilts of bone,
I smell your bodies, though you're bodiless,
And understand how easily you were doomed
By business failures, panics, medical mistakes
Which I have suffered for my soul's sake,
And miss you deeply in this middle age,
As nights when you'd go out like candlelight,
Leaving the smoke of your pipe and cigarette,
Your perfume and your after-shave cologne.

Immortality

Poems are written for the folks at home
Who scoffed at what we said in prose.
Poems are written for the folks who doze
In nursing homes, or villages of stone.

Poems are written for idealized others,
For the best traits in our fathers, mothers.
Poems are transcripts of our chromosomes
That once formed moving flesh and bone.

Poems are written sound by line by page
In momentary grief or fear or rage,
Knowing there is no one and no home.
Poems are written for their sake alone.

2. The Unholy Ground: A Sequence

0900

Sick of our stack of bills, we fled downtown
And watched silver speedboats whacking The Hudson,
T.V. helicopters shooting them, one by one,
While kayakers spun in the basin

At West Street, September 9, 2001.
Then the sun lit up our great glass phalli
Like flashbulbs popped on our doomed G.I'.s
And their sudden twins, their dead but cheerful Allies.

Blurry you watched this, feeling scared, depressed
That our stocks crashed; and so I tried to joke:
"*Sun Micro's* setting, but look what's coming next.
We don't have cancer, we're just old and broke."

A day or so later, at 0900 hours,
Our son called, "Click on the t.v.
A plane's just hit a World Trade Center tower."
"Grab a cab quick, here!" "Don't get panicky,"

And went up to his rooftop with his friends
And watched the next plane hit and watched Pompei,
Calling us on his cell phone, while we watched
Our financial Mecca turn first black, then gray;

Transfixed we watched, sleepless for days,
Searching for reassurance, courage, hope,
As if sitting *shiva* with two candles lit
For ashes scattered across Brooklyn Bay.

In the Restaurant

I'm served by Erica, badly exposed
To Chernobyl burning in those breakfast years,
Scrambling her cells to terrorist cells
Just miles from where my mother witnessed Hell.
"By smell," she says, "we're forced to witness this
Crematorium mixing bone and skin,
Spreading up here like metastasis...
And your son watched the two planes hit, and your
Brother-in-law escaped from a top floor?
So eat," she smiles like Mom, "You're getting thin."
And time and place collapse and the dust blows in.

Sleepwalkers

We necked on a bench
In Central Park
Till the trees gave up their leaves
To the unholy dark.

We stumbled to Sheep Meadow
And lay sideways down
Till the office lights went out
In the towers of midtown

Where terrorists roamed the streets
Casually as flirts,
Fingering vials of plague
Under New York Yankee shirts.

The autumn sky turned innocent,
Baby pink and blue,
And lit us in a rectangle
Of still green grass, black shoes.

We hopped a local train
To where the terrified stood,
And watched the smoke spread
As long as we could.

She Hands the Fire Captain a Photo

His name is Sean, he grins a goofy grin.
If you can find him, call me please.
His eyes are keen—he's seen the frown of Death!
He'll say my name—it's Beth—with his last breath.
He wears a silver cross, a V-shaped scar
Marks his left wrist—no, right!—from a bar fight,
Though he's just gentle as our Burmese cat.
If you can find his hand—or head!—please tell me that.
He loved these towers and his posh address.
He loved his view, his desk, his colleagues, friends.
He loves the East Side of Manhattan and the West.
He wears a double-breasted blazer, linen pants.
His tie is navy blue and never straight.
He smokes despite me, and he'll never dance.
His cell phone's broken and his rent is late.

For My Father

So this is how you felt during The War:
Our money smoke in the Market crash,
Your family of nine to support,
Baseball and Fred Astaire and the Big Bands
Stirring you momentarily like the smell of soap
You lathered with before your razor stropping,
Before you left the house at 4 A.M.
To lug ice till you came back making
Your ruined athletic body my lap,
While I watched Bernie smooth the crease in his army cap
And Sylvia on her Hope Chest draw in smoke
Before she'd leave for Dallas to her dumb G.I.
And had me grieving before I learned to grieve;
And the radio crackling Yiddish about more loss,
Stupendous loss which now we feel in scale,
Like those model aircraft carriers we made
For my toy planes; and while Mom cooked us supper
We knelt down on her linoleum floor
And, making zooming crashing sounds, we played.

Home

Dear souls, I've come back home to your worst fears,
My hatred of them, and our craziness
Which, like the terrorists, brought our rich structures down.
Some of my patients say that in their dreams
They see the Towers like their parents who
Broke down into abusiveness, neglect;
And see the airplanes carrying their own rage
—Oedipal, schizoid, borderline, the rest ...
All I know, from all my years of practice,
And what I've learned from self-analysis,
Is that you tried, you made mistakes, you did your best.

A current psychoanalytic joke is this:
What's the difference between an analyst
And a tailor? *Two generations.*
I'm like Grandpa Schechter in the cleaning store
Stitching the time in which I'd come to live
And what he knew by hand I'd come to learn
—How everything one builds in time must burn;
And I'm like Grandpa Willie who from Poland came
To beat up No One in the Polish bars,
His business dead as ash from his cigars.
Then his stocks crashed—and now The War,
And all that post-traumatic craziness I saw,
Taking it in my system like anthrax, plague;
And yet I was inoculated
By his example, by the care he gave,

As from your realm I sense you're showing me how
What I learned in childhood I am using now.

On the Cell Phone

You're in the Berkshires with your girlfriend—"Hi!" –
And, though our house has long been ruined and sold,
You're driving past it where our road is still
Turning, as always, burning red and gold,

And we're still in Manhattan, me and Mom,
Our Towers ancient rubble, smoking still,
And only seven years have passed, and we
Are drinking scotch to kill the coming chill.

And now that our retreat is gone (we knew
When we first bought it, it would come to this),
I'm singing *Heroism's* final song
About how lovers live from kiss to kiss

Until their autumn ends in killing snow
Falling on rooftops, boxcars, empty streets,
And you are bumping on our narrow road
And blowing kisses at our last retreat,

And in those windows, as in memory,
We're cooking, reading comics, writing poems
About this future that we knew would come,
Though we were safely sitting still at home.

Heroism is my musical drama done in 2000.

Windows on the World

We're nibbling at The Boat House, nearly dusk.
The Fall is burnt sienna, green and gold
In the high windows, around the lake,
And we are ages older—*never* old,

And so are our friends Mark and Marlene Stern
Who can't see the menace in the boats
—The rowers, anonymous in silhouette,
Casting nets of ripples for leaves that float

Like office paper before the Windows sank
Into a pit of toxins burning still.
Over the Upper West Side a plane banks.
The sky explodes in sunset. We feel chilled.

*Mark and Marlene Stern are the two leading characters in
Manhattan Carnival: A Dramatic Monologue. They re-
appear in the sequel *Dark Carnival: A Dramatic Monologue*
which forms section three of this book.

A Young Couple

A young couple comes to consult.
She's been exposed to anthrax
He wants to move to Chile,
And keep her safe with her family.
She wants to stay for his career.
What do I think? they ask,
Hugging and holding hands.
I think, I read this morning
That a couple they ferried
From Battery Park City
—Where they lived during the week—
To New Jersey where they drove
To their country house in Spring Lake,
Hired a baby sitter;
And, while she watched the Towers fall
In re-play, someone came
To their lawn and abducted
Their six-year-old daughter.
I think, Nothing is free now
—Time, safety, no certain choices.
The next patient, scared for her son,
Tells me there are no good parents left.
I disagree, I think—just helpless ones.

Phoenixes

(for Matt, later)

I thought that I was stronger than I am.
Death after death after death undid me.
My family seemed fresh sacrificial lambs.
Neither the present nor the future hid me,

And not like phoenixes they flew,
But like my old darlings, frightened, holding hands,
And like your high school girlfriend Amy who
Wore Death's unholy, pale gray wedding band.

Dear nephew, who in my mind won't grow old,
This is for you, for what you can't express,
Running as you did when the huge cloud rolled
For endless blocks. For Amy, please stay blessed.

Others

There is a timeless world in which they live,
In which old wounds are healed, right paths are taken,
In which they get exactly what they give,
In which they're loved and pampered, not forsaken.

Some waited too long to have a child,
Some to marry, crumple a dull career,
Some to leave a spouse whose voice was mild
But whittled down their soul from year to year.

And some turned wooden in their smiles and tongues
And some paced fragile hour to room to hour
And some took fire and smoke inside their lungs
And turned to powder in their office tower.

Oh, time ticks even in the infant's caul,
On mourners' wristwatches despite the Dead.
Somewhere God weeps, sorry for them all,
For what He's written, and for what She's said.

I sometimes see The God in Auschwitz smoke.
For years I watched Him fight internal fires.
At times I heard Her as a dirty joke
Old cronies told, maddened by desire

For sex and celebration, holy zest
For golden faith they'd swipe from churches,
Spilling with red wine, Montalcino's best,
For what intrigue can't seize, mere cash can't purchase:

The intimations in the dawning light
That waken in a poet freed from time
Only when passionate, when the mind is right,
Only when stressed, when the soul must scan and rhyme.

Half the Office

What seemed unnoticed when the towers fell
Now seems symbolic, lasting, luminous,
As if disaster cast a magic spell
On the merely simple, merely beauteous.

A print of Dürer's St. Jerome, a gift
Our oldest friends brought back from Amsterdam.
The meaning of his contemplation shifts
Now that they're ill. His forehead seems a lamp

By which I see our youthful lust and zest
After our dinner, after the end of light.
His eyes are dim, he needs a little rest
And so we lie back down and say goodnight.

Next my diploma, 1984,
For psychoanalytic training, and
A store-bought painting of a farm house door,
Blue like our Dutch Colonial, and land

With its luscious fruit trees—apple, peach, and plum,
Its grape arbor with its ancient moss-stained swing,
Its violet beds and staked delphiniums,
Its bluebirds, and its bluejays bickering.

Below the door, irises in profusion,
Stuffed in a basket colored copper, tin.
We bought our house in Time for its seclusion.
Our road once faced the Berkshires oldest inn

Where then only haystacks stood, their lights the stars
Our son would reach on tiptoe, trying to snatch
Fireflies, one hand Venus, one hand Mars.
It vanished as if Time blew out a match.

What is the meaning in this Chinese vase
Mom left, four scenes of mother and child
In daily tasks made fabulous as Oz?
The child is earnest, Mom is gracious, mild.

For me the meaning's green and porcelain white
And red and green and black with flecks of gold
And I am seven captive to delight
Though I am nearly sixty-two years old

And I can't mourn her, though I mourned the rest
Who died in clumps like those who disappeared
And when she fell down dead I got depressed
And lost myself in clouds of childhood fears.

The vase is calm in motion, glazed like hope
Covers me blindly with these simple themes,
Mother and child who will not have to cope
With what's beyond the realm of quiet dreams.

The Other Half

(for Frederick Turner)

I

WHAT HAPPENED now seems tragic but abstract,
Somewhat, after fear calm fear calm fear.
TV turns it to historical fact
As we complete the turning of the year,
As we switch channels on the Afghan Show.
The deli owner from Islamabad,
Who chattered about the NASDAQ and the DOW
Until they crashed with what few stocks he had,
Wears rhinestone flags in his sweater now
And asks me if I know the *Iliad*,
A poem which, like the Quran, defines our space.
I answer him, but what he understands
More than my words, the smile artificially lighting my face,
Is my tone: Hope despair, hope despair, hope,
As if we're shouting through Time's desert sands,
Two mock-knights: grace, disgrace, grace, disgrace, grace.
He sticks a cigarette between his lips.
He moves on to "Odysseus' Oases."
I have my mind on what I want to write.
We talk and gesture in this kind of stasis,
Lonely and frightening in this cave of quips.
I pay for my coffee, doughnuts, we shake hands.
He keeps the butt unlit and laughs, "Don't ask."
Allergic he remembers. Understand
In our New York City, such friends wear no masks.

"I wouldn't hurt you in a mask of smoke."
"Non-toxic," I laugh, "That's a *dirty* joke."
He nods, I nod, an Ishmael/Israelite,
Old comic strip characters, our bubbles
Emptying into question marks—contrite
Compassion for each other's troubles ...
I trudge back to my office where I'll write
Trauma and Symbolization in the dying light.

II

The room I write in is quiet as old age,
Rage dying, hope dying, despair dying.
I write by hand, slantwise on the page,
Sometimes closing my eyes and in pain sighing.
The carpet is a calming green and gold.
The couch, L-shaped, is Sheffield autumn brown.
Behind it is a table: cherry, maple, oak
Like the trees that protected the home we sold.
The air tingles, not with toxins—just jokes told
Like dreams, slips, associations. Here transference
And crazy actions make *symbolic* sense.
Resting on the table is a wooden swan
Also from our dining room—Fred, dream on—
And, colored like the good witch from *our* land in Oz,
Stargazer lilies bursting white and pink
In our home's earthenware, unbroken vase
Filled with spring water for the stems to drink;
In the window, a girl is lost in urban night,
Marching a keyboard to a metronome,
Above her Hopper lovers still as stone.
I glance at them when it gets hard to write

And at the statuette of white Quan Yin
Who, like my mother, is my soul's guardian;
Turn left, a stark white telephone
Where patients call in terrors from within.
Beside it is a radio whose news
Of terror gives in now to simple blues.
Above it is a vial of Klonopin.
Below it is a drawer with Cipro, masks,
Tunafish cans; M&M's red, white and blue,
My will, my passport, and my father's flask
For football whiskey—and what gifts have you?

I write and doze and write and doze again
Until the dawn blooms a purplish pink.
I wash and shave my stubble in the sink.
This book will take till I am sixty-four,
Three years from now—where will you be then?
I lie back on the couch, pick up my pen
And think of you reading this distraction.
I hope you find my ending ends in satisfaction,
Fitting you better than these crumpled clothes.
Before the world brings terror to my door,
I'll say, "Good morning, Fred," lie back and doze

The Return

After many deaths, after PTSD,
After nightmares and panics and flashbacks stopped,
We hopped the train downtown and dashed upstairs
To West Street, where our abandoned yacht was docked,
Spiffy, re-painted, engine repaired.
We took the ocean, turbulent and free.

And you in white slacks, bare feet, Oz-green
Scarf laughed in triumph on the slashing ride.
Your workout midriff slim, your arms outspread,
You danced with me, as we rocked side to side.
Two souls become one body, we sped
On sex and one red tank of gasoline

Until we anchored at our seafood haunt
And called for lobsters stuffed with clams.
But then came news of our burning towers
Where friends, now couples, jumped out holding hands.
We sat just listening, eating only Hours,
Terror crawling on our food like ants.

There was no way we could get back to twenty-eight,
You sitting here, pregnant with your news, beaming.
There was no way back even to West Street,
Its bridge collapsed like our engineering
A spirited return. Much too late,
We cracked our claws, slipped out the meat, and ate.

What Happened to Your Immortal City

This was your silver, immortal city,
Although you knew all empires fall
From their own inattention.
But not this glorious Democracy:
New York, New York, although Frank Sinatra
—Who is he, who will he be?—is dead,
And, for now, Madison Square Garden
Waits, still, in this new millennium,
For Willis Reed—who is he?—to limp on court,
And Mayor Giuliani and Mayor LaGuardia
(For whom an airport is named) are standing
In two downtowns, smiling and looking brave.
And you write this on some muggy day,
The sky almost a blank of clouds,
And the leaves in your garden still
Insistently green, and this moment of pain
Relieved by a childhood memory
Of the sound of sixty-year-old rain.
So you pick up an old man's book,
Robert Penn Warren's *Rumor Verified,*
Which you read as a warning when you were exuberant,
Where he asks, "Is all wisdom learned too late?"
And he says, "The time comes when you count the names,"
Or name them simply, even Buddy Young,
That pint-sized halfback for the football Yankees,
Or Yogi Berra squatting—do you know him?—
In his iron mask, or Dan Dailey
Dancing on a screen, black and white,

Before your lifetime, or further back
The mute Charlie Chaplin who seemed unfunny,
Or before that an anonymous clerk
In a stovepipe hat, bearded—what decade? –
Blessing someone, a dead little girl
Who, as an old woman, remembered many details ...
And now helicopter blades
Cut your reveries, and the threats of this time,
And the impermanence of this place
Bring you back to Penn Warren
Sitting under a tree somewhere south
And describing, "News that the afternoon burns bright.
It blazes in traumatic splendor."
Ah, you were never alone, not like this
Among your loved ones, your enemies.
Not quite exactly, not like this.

Journey's End

The hero's journey is circuitous,
And brings him home alone,
Quite quiet in the dawn,
To fight what's hooded, barbarous,
And tries to take possession of his soul.
And if he prays to no One marvelous,
The spirit in him keeps what No One stole.
The spirit in him rises weeping, whole.

Manhattan Music

It's Easter morning in Manhattan, now
Millennium plus two; still Spring,
That ancient reassuring wonder, where
Clock radios play Vivaldi, wrens
Twitter from trees to clotheslines, jets
Reverberate, couples bicker or moan,
Dogs bark, babies scream, an opera singer
Melodiously clears her throat
To the trumpeting of fire engines
And the bassooning of tugboats
—Incidental music, random, bold
Harmonies, waking Manhattan's soul.

3. Dark Carnival: A Dramatic Monologue

N.B. In *Manhattan Carnival* Mark Stern wakes up depressed, to an empty marriage bed after having a one-night stand. He and his wife Marlene have split up because (among many reasons) he's wanted to have a child and she hasn't.

Manhattan Carnival, set in the seventies, is Mark's journey through a carnival-like Manhattan to find her. He does, and the book-length poem (and verse play) ends with Mark and Marlene having sex and conceiving a child.

Here, in *Dark Carnival,* it's thirty-one years later. Their child Jill has lost her husband Jack in the World Trade Center disaster. It begins with Mark again waking up to an empty bed. This time Mark takes a journey through a changed New York to try to find not only Marlene but also his widowed daughter.

Stylistically lines and many passages are in parallel and contrast to lines and passages in Manhattan Carnival. Though I say something like that in the Afterword, this is much more precise.

Dark Carnival

Mark Stern Wakes Up

Get up, Mark Stern, it's summer, spring, it's fall,
And winter's coming fast; the caterwaul-
Ing geese, heading for Miami Beach
Fly in a V, perfectly out of reach,
As Jack, twirling bacon on a fork,
Called on his cell phone—then flew from New York
Over New Jersey, south to God knows where,
A soul in freedom, once a millionaire
Broker with Morgan Stanley, handsome Jack,
Sensitive Jack. Mourning won't bring him back.
    Get up, he's gone, marriage is for the birds.
Marlene would get the fury in those words.
It's only six o'clock, Marlene. Marlene,
Where are you? Why did you leave this magazine
—Opened to Jack and Jill in their wedding clothes,
Jill still innocent, a single white rose—
On the bathroom sink? What does this note say?
"Meet us for breakfast at Marty's Café
Before Jill goes to work. She's not depressed,
Just lonely. Just shave, Mark. Hurry. Get dressed."
    The sky is cloudless, baby blue, pristine
As 9/11 blue. These streets are clean
As if the Swiss had scrubbed them. Are *they* free
And fearless, freed by prosperity?
But we assert old glory with new flags

That hang from every canopy—like tags,
Multicolored, from flower boxes. *Good Luck.*
Happy Birthday—from every car and truck,
And flags on these brownstone steps and windowsills
—Commemorating Jack and cheering Jill:
We love you, Jill— you must stay brave and sane;
Let's roll, let's live, red, white and blue—and plain-
Ly happy, plainly innocent like Jack,
And if there is another, worse attack ...?
   This street is festive, though it's half for lease
Or sale; the other half insists that peace
Will stay, that we'll stay hopeful and strong-willed.
This brownstone's steps hold eight big pumpkins filled
With flowers. *That* one's ready for December,
Its windows sprayed with snowflakes and "*Remember!*"
And cardboard reindeers, paper Oz-green sleds
With Santas waving off our daily dread,
And doors are opening, parents taking kids
To school, *as usual,* Marlene as we did,
Jill laughing at me always making faces
My fake astonishment, my sweet grimaces.
And here are wincing movers bringing in
A padded grand piano, legs stork-thin,
The owner with a Snugglie like you wore,
And we will always keep her safe—we swore.
All flags are flapping in a sudden wind.
Fate sat Jill on a Ferris wheel and spinned.

Marty's Café

I walk to Marty's neighborhood café.
Its lettering: *Manhattan Night And Day.*
Its window frames the families of the ill
Around the corner in the hospital,
Where single deaths will leave them stupefied;
The unemployed lost in the classifieds,
The Hopper greenish-faced insomniacs
Nursing their orange juice, their rounded backs
Like wicked monkeys in the Land of Oz.
The hang-overs, exhausted with the blahs.
  I'm asking Marty, "Where's Marlene, where's Jill?"
"Check the Lost and Found. Gimme the bill.
She drank a quart of vodka and she drowned."
The fat prof with his red and drunken face
Sneers, "Marky/Mocky. No Jews in this place."
Marty yanks him from his booth. "Get out!" (Applause.)
And flings him through the door. "He sits and snores
All night quoting me 'De Ride Her,' and 'Backed In.'"
Marty shrugs, "What's 'Derrida/Bakhtin',"
He scrawls on these napkins, then goes back to sleep?
I should have tossed him out before, the creep.
"But everyone's a family now …" "And Jill?"
"They came. She cried. They left … That greasy grille
Is burning sausage … Clean it up, you jerk!
Is there another chef here out of work?"
The crowd laughs, startling at clouds of smoke.
"When you've been shocked, you need a little joke,"
Marty slaps my back, "You go down, they go up."
  He sits me down, pours coffee in my cup,
Slides in beside me, "How's she doing, Jill?
I love that little blond, that daffodil.

When you first moved here, she was six-years-old.
We didn't realize then that time was gold."
"After Jack Kennedy, where do you go?"
But Marty doesn't get the name's allusion.
"Our President," I clear up his confusion,
"And Jack, my son-in-law, both seemed the same
Ideal to me and Marlene." "What a shame!"
Marty gets up, it's too much sentiment.
He blinks to show he's gotten what I meant.
    I'll call you on the cell phone, call at Jill's …
No answers, my hand shakes, the coffee spills.
The waitress rushes over with a glass of Seltzer.
Jack's real name wasn't Kennedy, but "Meltzer."

The Block

    The stain has formed a bull's-eye on my chest.
I'll walk to Jill's apartment. God, I'm stressed.
So I begin to jog. I'm out of shape.
I want to run through time, slant back, escape
My body to our best time, Jill at six
Subtracting her first-grade arithmetics
On the steps of the World Financial Tower's
Winter Garden, after shopping there for hours.
    My lungs are bruised; my ribs are tightened belts,
My eyes are cuts, my sinuses are welts.
I'm slowing down to our old block in Yorkville,
Before we split up, then were healed by Jill.
This block we lived on long has lost its stores
Whose names I don't remember anymore,
Just *Happy's,* that obscene and smiling Greek,
Strong with his garlic but his wine was weak,

His Swedish meatballs (when we still ate meat)
Better than *Café du Soir's* across the street.
    Now Nick the nephew owns the flower shop.
His brother was a World Trade Center cop
In the old days. I wave to him. He grins,
Gestures with his fingers that I must come in.
His waist and hairline are his uncle's now.
His uncle's worry-lines thicken his brow.
Amidst the small-talk, "Yes, my brother died."
Ten floors below Jack. "A hero, yep, he tried
Bringing his second trip of rabbits down."
I show him Jill, dressed in her wedding gown.
I quote, "A white rose, just for you, Marlene."
He smiles at what his uncle said, sixteen
Again, when he cut tulips at that table.
"My older brother was as good as Abel."
He weeps as if these thirty years were dreamed.
And weren't they, while these mad Mullahs schemed?
    Memory survives here. Happy isn't dead.
The green Gristede's pear turns back to red.
I shake Nick's hand and walk across the street
To where you're shopping pregnant, while you eat
Doughnuts and coffee from your shopping cart.
I'm back, Marlene, at our second start.
    Stella's fruit stand—do you remember her?—
Where you would buy big home-grown cucumbers
We called, "Stella's fresh dildos." Now she's married.
"Hello," *you ugly twins.* Stella looks harried
But she's still beautiful beneath the weight
She's gained, still crass Sicilian, "Grab that crate,
Cafone! ... Give a peck to my Marlene ...
The youngest one is twelve, these two fifteen ...
Hey, tell that driver he can't double-park!

He'll find my bite goes deeper than my bark.
My husband is a fireman, he's healthy
—For now. But no one on this block stayed wealthy,
Not even the gypsy fortune-teller 'Joan,'
Né *Shushi*. She's still up there on her own."
She points above her to the second floor.
"I'll bet in this economy she'll whore.
She's lost all in the market, all her dough,
Like all of us. You're smart though, Mark ... Oh, no!"
She pats my face, goes in to fill her bins.
Upstairs I hear Joan's gypsy violin.
Remember how in summer she would play
Through opened windows, drawing in her prey?

    And Good Health still is standing there:
Same size, same clerk, same friendless stare.
And here's two beggars, Jill's age with guitars,
Costumed like hippies leaning on parked cars,
Plucking, singing—they point—for me, our song,
Yesterday. "Come on, dude, sing along."
One's shuddering as if to fight the cold
Hands of the terrorists' sign-language: *Death.*
But joy still trembles on their twinning breath.
Oh, bring back the '60's. Bring back George and John.
Let Ringo's beat go on forever, "On and On."
Imagine peace and beauty and the truth,
Despite P.C.'s, Marlene, we're still the youth
That led the marches and the freedom rides,
Candlelight marches, arms linked, side by side.

    And in our old apartment I see two
Lovers embracing, just like me and you,
Waving when I wave: *This is Old New York!* ...
The cell phone's dead. Marlene, we have to talk
About the future which was *Yesterday.*

Our wallpaper's still up there, silver-gray.
Many sunny days we'd have a marathon
Of sex and food—those hours were halcyon.
Marlene, I love you, even on Voice Mail.
Oh, we succeeded where we couldn't fail.
Even though poor here, we were glutted with hope;
Then rich when I wrote television soaps.
And though I wound up with my plays obscure,
We lived in time here, sexual, cocksure.
    Up there those lovers' bodies now are where?
Naked on the floor, in our rocking chair,
Or up against our wall in our embrace?
They can't exterminate the human race!
They're back, our shadows, dressed but whole.
He's juggling two glasses, she a bowl
Of Cezanne fruit, pears bluish in this light.
Each day's a gift. They're toasting out of sight,
Retreating to our past. *Here's to Yesterday!*
I tip the "hippies" and I walk away.

Central Park

    I must get moving. Where is there to go
From Once Upon A Time And Long Ago?
Where is our future, where are you, Marlene? ...
This phone is dead. It needs another quarter.
Maybe you're across town with our daughter.
    I'm running past the Met, through Central Park
Where roller bladers swerve as pit bulls bark,
Where in slow motion men do *ta-kwon-do*
Beside a white-faced, statuesque Pierrot,
Where bike messengers stop for basketball.

One flies high for a lay-up, eight feet tall.
The rim shudders like a jet's shock wave
And Jack, the Brown star, lies still in his grave
And men who've lived ten, twenty years past him
Frolic in softball, past the shuddering rim.
I pick my pace up towards the sound of wrens
Flitting like whole notes, puffed with oxygen.
Maintenance workers mount their yellow machines,
Their uniforms fresh-laundered aquamarine.
The wrens rise *acopella* from the throat
Of some soprano. Turn left to the Moat
Where swans under Belvedere's Castle float,
And willows bend, and maples tinged with red
Give the illusion no one's really dead.
    I suck my wind in for a baby carriage.
"Sorry," I'm dashing to my daughter's marriage.
But they are posting on this gray dust trail:
Black horses, Jill all female, Jack all male,
And I'm content, our life's work moving well.
Who knew this trail would lead poor Jack to hell
The next day when, at 8:46, he fell?
And now the time's the same! One-two, I pick up pace
As if I'm running in a frantic race
With Nick's late brother up a smoky stair,
While Jill's with Marlene, lost in her despair.

Racing to Columbus

    I'm running out to where the planets pause
Red, white, and blue, obeying man-made laws,
Behind the Rose Planetarium's façade.
When we four saw it first, we oo'd and ah'd,

Not knowing then our universe would stop.
If only Jack was helped down by Nick's cop,
Instead of telling Jill on his cell phone,
"They say to stay inside … I'm not alone
Or scared." And then he called her from the roof.
I see them high and laughing, hoof by hoof
Their horses kicking gray smoke through the air.
No helicopter answered poor Jack's prayer.
I squeeze my eyes shut till he disappears.
I run against the light when traffic clears,
Eyes more than open to the living stream
Of business people walking in a dream
Of downtown where their buses, subways go,
Armed with a briefcase or portfolio
Against another cowardly attack.
In them the future's slowly coming back.

   I'm on Columbus, Brave New World, where shops
Open with pushed-up gates and shaking mops,
And young clerks happy at their One More Day,
As all New Yorkers fight off fear, decay
Of hope, of optimism, youth and luck.
The next attack we'll all be horror-struck.
But now, for now, Columbus shows his smile.
I slow down, having run for two, three miles.
And here's her building, here I ring the bell.
Please answer, Jill, these notes for Philomel.
But no one answers. There's another phone …
The Voice Mail picks up. It's Jack's baritone.
"Meet me," I say, "—It's Dad *ad nauseam*—
At Barney Greengrass's on Amsterdam.

Jackie

I need "The Sturgeon King," his sturgeon, herring, lox,
His waiters with their '60's faces clocks
Telling their time's all ours, Margritte-surreal;
Their lovely gestures as they bring my meal
Of pea soup, baked salmon, bagel with *shmear*
Parodies childhood, warns old age is near.
There is no comfort in their worn-out care
—Our grandchild's tiny soul was stopped mid-air.
But Jill will get re-married once she's whole.
I tap my spoon against the pea soup bowl.
One-two, one-two, each rounded shape's a clock.
A white fish lies down on the chopping block.
Head goes, tail goes until it's tender meat.
I need fresh air, I need the human street
Where pregnant women waddle, Jill grows strange ...
I drop a ten, not waiting for the change.
I knock my plate down. "Jackie, get the broom!"
In our dead years there is a baby boom
And "Jackie's" father is a lucky man,
Dead or alive ... Jill does the best she can,
And my need for a future doesn't matter.
    A stranger sits where I sat. "*Kvetch* me a platter
Of that white fish, sliced *challah*, and a coke."
Jackie guffaws. My fill-in's told a joke.
And jokes and sex and pregnancies go on.
The future's here, although their future's gone.
The crowd in motion counters me with hope,
Their colored clothes a child's kaleidoscope.
    The street's now full of children off to school.
I enter them, swim in a wading pool.
She lugs a briefcase much too big for her.

He throws his hands up at a jabberer.
She beats her chest and howls like an ape.
He shifts his jacket to a Batman cape ...
In those brief years they couldn't have a child.
They're greeting "Grandpa." Grandpa is beguiled
But weighted down with quarters—all is changed.
Where are you Jill,' *this* makes me half-deranged.

The Garbage Drummer

    I need to pump endorphins, jog to where
The park ends in The Plaza and Pierre,
Where Jack proposed, where Jill said, "Yes, No, Yes,"
Where tourist couples, free of our distress
Climb into flowered horse-drawn carts.
The drivers, Slavs or Greeks, talk from their hearts
Like young Venetian boatmen that they met
On their month-long honeymoon. I'm sweat-
Ing and my chest hurts, Marlene, or my heart,
My lungs, my stomach, yes no yes, a fart
Passersby glare at. I huddle at a phone.
"Hey, man, get out. This phone booth's not your own!"
Someone taps me with drumsticks on my shoulder.
"It can't be *you,* thirty years older!"
"What the fuck, man, I need to make my call."
"You drummed on garbage cans, against that wall.
'It's Krupa now, you recognize that beat?'
I stood there, clapping Bravo, on my feet
After I watched you, right *there,* on that bench."
"Hey, man, you've farted, what a fucking stench!"
"'You're brilliant, man,' I said, 'so why this gig?'"
'They catch you forging checks when you get big,'

You said." "I said, you said, I said, you said!"
He taps my shoulder, tap taps past my head
To tap that beat out on the phone booth's side
Made of plastic. "Hey, dude, take a buggy ride!"
He can't stop rapping with that same old skill.
I stuff his shirt with a five-dollar bill.
Then duck to watch him play the telephone.
"I *know* you, man, your wrinkles say you've grown
Way past me." He laughs, "Baby, slap me five!"
He twirls his sticks—our past is here alive!—
And we high-five, "Hey!" smiling at each other.
"I'll to drink to *us,* with this five bucks, my brother!"

The "V""

I smile goodbye, I've had a sudden thought:
When wild, Jill winds up at the tennis court
In Queens, at Fila, where she first met Jack.
She hit fast forehands but he hit them back
Game after game, set after set. The match
Ended—with *both* winners. Marlene, let me catch
My breath, one-two, deep down the subway stairs.
I jump the turnstile. "Buddy, where's your fare,
Your Metro card?" "I have to catch the 'V.'"
The cop stops, door closed, furious at me.
I walk from car to car. I'll get arrested.
Two years ago I'd think, This train's infested
With psychos, addicts, beggars, thieves and whores,
And students, old men, blind men—just the poor's
Group portraits, just the salvaged human race:
Apostrophes, all standing in Jack's place.
Now all of us are riding in this V,
Substitute geese, except the geese were free.
I exit, run upstairs, run seven blocks,
I'm burping salmon and my tongue is lox.
Until I stop—dry mouth—before the skyline,
All glass and silver in the white sunshine:
The Chrysler Building and The Empire State
Declare to airplanes, *Man, not God, is Great.*
The U.N.'s green, illusory as Oz
Where one commits not murder but *faux pas*
And anti-semitism is P.C.
As if it is a University,
Our own *madrassa* made of tinted glass,
Concrete and steel and cemetery grass.
    Cruising the river is a lone patrol.

A cop is stirring coffee with a roll.
A diver tumbles down the freezing river.
The cop on board signals the man will shiver
Despite his suit, his goggles—he is scared
A mine's been planted. But the man's been dared
By bullies who would sneak in underwater.
I have to run, I have to find my daughter.

Kirk

   I trudge up Fila's steps as if I've played
A tournament in sweat pants made of suede.
I ask the desk clerk, "Have you seen Marlene?"
"Huh?" "Or Jill?" She squints as if the name's obscene.
She's clean, she has been purified by death.
"You okay? Pop, it's time to catch your breath."
"Kirk was my daughter's coach. Her name's Jill Stern."
She turns the book to show me—"Kirk's with Fern.
They're on court ten. So he'll be done at ten."
I turn my watch to her. Her eyes are Zen,
Are tranquil, unlike Jill's wide eyes all frantic.
Has she lost no one over the Atlantic
Where shadows of a thousand souls formed V's?
For what? For them—*Al Immortality?*
Three thousand souls—not theirs!—were heaven sent.

   This girl is smiling, she's still innocent.
"Slap, slap, I'm sorry. That clock says that Kirk
Gets off at noon. I've *just* come here to work.
Till yesterday I lived in L.A. time.
"*Yesterday,*" I linger. "Huh?" "Forget it, I'm
Also living in two time-zones. I'm

Two *years* behind, looking to find Jack and Jill."
"Mother Goose," she laughs, "that's Early L.A. time
—When Mom recited *Jack 'n Jill* in rhyme:
'Jack and Jill went up the hill to fetch a pail of water.
Jack fell down and broke his crown and...'" "Please, my daughter ..."
"And Jill came tumbling after!" "Kirk!" "Mark Stern! ...
Where's Jill? ... How's Jill?" He's warm, I'm taciturn.
"She's fine. She's better." I'm not here.
"She walked off court with Jack the Financier.
Jack and Jill," he grins. "I coached them both as kids."
Long pause. "Oh no!" Kirk lowers his eyelids.
His lights go out, Fila is downtown black.
"I should have guessed. My God, my God, God, Mark!"
Kirk holds his mouth, he hugs me, pats my back.
New Yorkers speak in code since the attack.

Times Square

　　Back on the V, I'm headed nowhere fast,
The faces blur, as if we've all been gassed.
But we're on 51rst and safe, my stop.
I'm smiling at a different transit cop
And running upstairs, as I've done all day.
I turn back when I hear a rock band play
Yesterday, of course, New York City's song.
A crowd forms, and with them I sing along.
Soon everyone is laughing, crying, silent-
Ly thinking we're are loving and non-violent.
But blaring Death won't leave our town alone.

The band leader passes the microphone
And we sing fragments of "New York, New York."

I raise my fingers, *V*, a tuning fork
And from this chorus swaying underground
One pure voice rises, one angelic sound,
Wordless, enduring passion breaking free
Above the traffic gridlock's horns' cacophony.
   I'm brightened by the sunlight in Times Square,
Our Disney World, this playwright's downfall, where
We sold, when broke, the touring Japanese
Steel Twin Towers, tin Empire States,
Miniature cabs, New York license plates,
Statues of Liberty—cheap souvenirs.
Reduced Manhattan harmlessly disappears
From huge stores, small stands, *psst psst* knock-off bags
Winos lug, made of American flags.
This Times Square is a souk, a carnival
Where tattooed druggies mix with biblical
Preachers and peep-show businessmen who lurk
For quick fixes before their pin-striped work,
Among the hawkers of fake jewelry,
Americans Al Immortality,
Makes prey—Mozombiques and Vietnamese
And Pakistanis, Malis, Japanese
—All splendid decking out the goods we'd sell,
All multicolored, every infidel,
And Saudis, Yemenis, and Sudenese.
America is packed in a valise,
Each opens, not a dirty bomb, a vial
Of smallpox—there's no murder in the smile
Of missing teeth or, if they're lucky, gold.
They're all New Yorkers, flashy, chatty, bold
Beneath huge billboards selling underwear
On gorgeous nudes, huge sculpture in mid-air,
And ads for scotch and DVD's and slacks.

This is what Al Immortality attacks.
The whole square trumpets, *This is Liberty,*
"These teeming masses yearning to be free"
Of amputation, clitorectomy;
For what these peddlers joyfully declare
Is real Americana, *buy, compare*
Manhattan Music, passionately rare.

The Village

Jefferson's Market's Tower's clock strikes one.
I'm where Jill works—where *he* lived ... God, I've run
For miles. I peer in restaurants to see
If Jill's at lunch ... I'm lost in lunacy
—The dream I had that woke me up at six
Was set right here, you up to your old tricks
Of, when we had those troubles, walking out
Without a goodbye note, a call to shout,
"Fuck your affairs, Mark Stern, forget a kid."
Instead in silence you did what I did,
And I remember... *Mark Stern, let this go,*
This *Once Upon A Time And Long Ago!*"
Except I'm standing right across his street ...
You're sixty now. History won't repeat.
We fought breast cancer, Jack's death, 9/ll.
Your lover's name up there was Morris Levin!
    I'm back now thirty years when he drops dead,
You naked, Marlene, panicked in his bed.
Is *this* why I've been frantic? Jill's okay
Most days. *Go, time-bound thought, take thee away,*
And think of Marlene struggling to give birth,
And struggling now to bring Jill back to Earth!

I'm struck by wonder at *this* blessed hour
—Its flower shop, its every living flower,
This smoke shop with its hash pipes, magazines,
This costume shop with this year's Halloween
Masks of Bin Laden and Saddam Hussein,
Crusader helmets, swords and balls and chains,
S&M costumes, now political
—Not merely harmless, merely sexual.

Lady Madonna's

And now I'm gasping where—you'll never guess ...
Lady Madonna's where you bought that dress
For you and Jill, innocent in your womb.
Where you shut marriage out, you now made room.
I've come here through two time zones, through time's waste
To where you grew our baby, we grew chaste,
And life grew calm with not one day of friction.
And now it seems those days were just a fiction
And all reality just 9/11.
Remember when we'd sing, Jill, *My Blue Heaven?*
And how we swore she'd grow with no regrets
Like ours? Their hours, their up and down duets
Were Mozart rondos, Mozart minuettes.
    I'm slowing to another time zone—"3ʳᵈ"
And "B", a movie set trucked off, absurd-
Ly gone, my favorite childhood shops,
Where we'd read *Archies*, chewing lollipops,

Munching on pretzels downed with soda pops,
In tenements where mothers shook out mops
From windows, snowing ashes on us all.
Just household ashes falling as we'd crawl
From snow forts backwards, red boots, soaking hats,
Or jump in fresh heaps, flipping acrobats,
Or cram like circus clowns on home-made sleighs.
"Où sont les neiges d'antan," our yesterdays?

Lenny

    I've grabbed a cab to Katz's Deli where
I watch us young, ambitious—a gorgeous pair,
Gorging on hard salami, corned beef, fries,
Playwright and actress swallowing rage and lies
Before we married … Jill is thirty-one
Today! "Just tuck a burnt frank in a bun
With mustard, heap on sauerkraut, relish …"
"Take it slow. Standing at this grille is hellish."
I know this man. It's Lenny who wrote plays
We staged at Actors Studio. The praise
Critics gave him! He spurned movies, t.v. scripts.
And now he scrubs the floor where fat has dripped?
I want to recognize him, squeeze his hand.
I want to yank his sweaty gray headband,
—A napkin knotted—slipping on his brow.
I want to ask him, "Lenny, how could you
Of all the playwrights in our group debut
Corned Beef instead of *"Here Go Sailor Jack,"*
His satire on the nuclear attack
Kennedy almost launched in '62.
And what is Jack to me, and me to you?

I thank him for his gift and leave a tip.
He laughs and mutters, "Stern, you're still a pip.
And did they turn *your* hot plays into dogs?
Did bad directors *shtick* those dialogues
You stitched with such sure *Shtickomythia?*
They stuck it to me for my whole Korea.
He mocks his future which has long been past:
"He who stays sincere, enthusias-
Shtick about Art is like the terrorist
Who scripts a tape, like each smug egotist
Who smirked in Actors Studio with us."
I slap him five, and walk out stuffed, depressed.
We were so talented. But we're still blessed,
Not like those high with Jack in that Smash Hit.
Why did we snarl in rages, eat that shit
In that Stage Deli after you'd audition?
For years High Art was *our* religious mission.

Mulberry

Mulberry Street where Jill would go to shop
For olives, dried cod, freshly-killed veal chops.
It's San Genarro's Feast with tourists snacking
Calzone, Sicilian Pizza, smacking
Their stomachs, hearts, stretching their arteries
With candied apples and ricotta cheese
Sloshed down with red wine, white wine, cider, beer.
Here thoughts of 9/11 disappear
Down their digestive tracts they'll carry back
To Bay Ridge, Philly, Stamford, Hackensack.
Tonight this street will be a feast of lights,
Rose-colored, Oz-colored, yellow, blue, and white,

With belting by Dean Martin, Pavorotti
And karioka by Lone Wolf and Wild Coyote
And old men playing gin who smoke and cough,
Their drunken *moglies* taking "something off"
—A scarf, a shawl they'll wrap around the face
Like Moslem women, dancing with studied grace.
    I walk around them, out to Chinatown.
I'm in a maze. I have to get downtown,
Way past the herbal tea and noodle shops,
Way past the Chinese mothers wielding mops
To chide their children who've been Westernized.
They're straight lines, dots—they're all apostrophized
Immigrants who've survived foul cargo ships
And spare ribs smeared with sweet and sour dips
And chickens burned to pimpled skin and bones
And pretty peddlers burned by Time to crones
And old men, young men hawking watches, rings,
And lit-up Yo Yo's circling on white strings
Around The World, or Sleeping as we learned
When children, ignorant that towers burn
And crumble like tall parents unprepared
For what we dreamed of but we hadn't dared
To fully fantasize about. I sprint
To New York City's government
Buildings—The Court House, Police Plaza, City Hall
Where lawyers march, where vagrants slide down walls
Where Mayans play what sounds American
On tambourines and home-made pipes of Pan.

The Smoker

J & R records and appliance stores
Still stand across from City Hall Park, galore
With packs of CD's gift-wrapped, DVD's,
Digital cameras, plasma-thin t.v.'s,
All pointing to a future—Christmastime
When Trinity Church's ancient bells will chime
That we know nothing, though we've heard it all:
The cell phone call, and then the dying fall.
    Between the stores, a hardware store's display:
Four photos stand on a flag turned gray.
Four handsome firemen, still unterrified.
Four young Jacks. One's son, smiling, at his side
Zooming model airplanes that they've made.
One with his daughter hawking lemonade,
Down on one knee, arm around her shoulder.
One a boy, Neverever older.
And one just sturdy, happy, gaze naïve.
His photo on this flag seems make-believe,
An artifact among his FDNY cap,
His firehouse glued, red-circled on a map
Of Old New York that seems his Land of Oz,
His tiny Engine 6 with Santa Claus,
Wise, familial in the driver's seat,
His ladder stuffed with candies, bakery treats,
All miniature, freed from gravity,
Suspended in mid-air, as Jack would be.
"Where are you Jack on this red, white, and blue?"
I say aloud. "And where are Jill and you?"
    Behind me someone lights a cigarette,
His squinting, burning eyes in silhouette.
"You see those tourist lines around St. Paul's

Chapel of Trinity Church? They've stopped to scrawl
Three thousand phrases in the present tense
On banners, bedsheets, stuffed in its iron fence:
'We love,' they start, 'We hope,' they start.' 'God bless!'
Over three thousand signatures, more or less,
Their sentimental verses on oak tags,
Their sentimental floral wreathes with flags."
He lifts his trembling fingers in a V.
"Their sentiments of our democracy:
Bedsheets imprinted with Miss Liberty,
Lifting her torch, her profile, strong, severe,
Washington on his horse and Paul Revere
And our bald eagle looking for a perch,
All wedged in the iron fence around the church.
I know you've seen it, here, there, seen it all,
Life's paraphernalia and life's folderal."
I nod, he smiles, I nod, he smiles again.
"I know you're mourning, we're two angry men."
He blows a perfect smoke ring, then another:
In Old English, "*Thaïs Oferaoder...*'
This too will pass, this too will fade away.
My daughter was an English Ph.D.
When I was sick, she'd quote that line to me.
And now she's, buddy ... What a goddamn joke,
And now I'm burning in these clouds of smoke.
My wife took pills ... And yours?" I shake my head.
"What do these tourists know about our dead!
Like me you're puffing, screaming here with why's,
Watching my smoke rings fill with fireflies.
Blink on, blink off, Life's here, Life's there, Life's gone ...
I'll see you buddy. Sorry. I'll move on."
He wags his fingers in goodbye to me,
Then whirls them at the tourists violently.

"She flew off from her perch on 53,
My pretty goose, my pretty Ph.D.
And was your daughter pregnant?" "No," I say.
"I only lost my son-in-law that day."
He grins as if I've told a dirty joke,
Then storms off in a tiny cloud of smoke.

Our Tourist Site

   Finally I'm at Our Tourist Site
Where our living struck by a meteorite
Turned into ghosts, hovering over a hole
Half-a-mile wide, rummaging for their souls
Now that these yellow bulldozers have done
Shoveling their bones, steel, iron, ton by ton
Onto dump trucks, ferries, and landfills.
I want to hollar, "Help me, Marlene, Jill.
Barriers must rise around our agonies,"
Like this fence keeps the crowd alive and free
Of ghosts that lurk here, searching for their hands,
Their pens, their yellow pads, their wedding bands,
The frames holding pictures of Jack and Jill.
   I must reach water, I am faint, I'm ill.
What were those lines? *"I am sick, I must die,*
God have mercy on us." Here's where Jack lies.
And I am running out to where I bet
The two of you are sitting—*Never Forget!* –
And all this horror now is fenced and tame
Where we searched frantic, screaming out Jack's name.
We searched the hospitals, its psych wards, morgues,
The blind blundering through Chaos with their dogs.

The Winter Garden

The World Financial Center seems intact
As if only its shadow was attacked.
A clerk politely gives out slick brochures
And perky guides lift placards up for tours:
"Are we all present?" There's no missing past.
I join them crossing the skyway, aghast
That these same figures crumpling at St. Paul's
Are snappy G.I. Joes and Barbie dolls,
Nodding and flirting, stopping for ice cream cones:
Vanilla, chocolate, steel and glass and stone.
    I hear an ancient melody begin.
It's *Earth Angel* played by two violins
And cello, coming from the Winter Garden:
Jill's holy place, and our Forest of Arden
With Oz-green palms—the same as when we'd come
(Subtracting years, red circling the sum)
When we were young, when Jill was only six,
Happy, comic, lost in arithmetics:
2002 subtract to '78
Before we multiplied—to Heaven's gate,
Before she finished first grade, second, third,
When all was future, nothing was absurd.
Nothing from nothing makes no cents—no sense!
And Nothing rose behind that awful fence,
Reducing Jill by fractions. Oh, dear Jill
Before you grew ... Marlene, when you were ill
We thought that time had ended, all was lost.
    But now you're here—of course!—adding the cost
With Jill, sitting where Jack again proposed,
And Jill smiled *Yes,* then like our child she dozed,
Head on his shoulder, as she leaned on mine ...

Here with Earth Angel, sitting with the fine-
Ly polished marble, rose and tragic gray.
"I should have guessed. I looked for you all day.
I've called, I've searched Manhattan—everywhere."
But Jack was nowhere in the laundered air,
Jill tells me with a mocking grin—*Despair!*
This place is undespairing—it's swept clean
Of Death and violence. Jill, my dear Marlene …
"What are you seeing, Jill? *What* did you say?"

Jill

   "I've come to mourn him here and, as we've prayed,
We've heard rock music classically played.
I see Jack dancing in a masquerade
With Lady Death—black dress, black hat, white plume
Uptown, crosstown, and in our living room.
Her bends her low. She tries to kiss his lips.
He keeps her distant in a graceful dip.
The music swells, and they are out of sight.
I call him, 'Jack, come back to say Goodnight.'
This song is from your time, a haunting melody
My ghost, *'My darling, save the last dance for me.'*
   Now Jill sits, small, beside me on a stair.
I see Jack dancing, molecules of air
Under the Winter Garden's mosque-like dome
Now cleared of rubble … "Daddy take me home
By cab, let's see our skyline as we drive
As it still stood when Jack was still alive:
The Chrysler Building and The Empire State.
We ate this island whole on our first date
From the Brooklyn Bridge to the George Washington.

84

Please help me get up with the setting sun
Smearing our skyline with a blinding sheen."
    Come on, let's take our baby home, Marlene.
Let's flag a cab or gypsy limousine.
Let's take her home, to thirty years and back
Before another terrorist attack
(Their bodies shaved, their eyes all deadened black)
Attempts to make our skyline disappear.
Let's seize the day, this night, this year.
Let's seize Thanksgiving, Christmas ... Do you hear
That segue, bows drawn slowly as they play.
They innocently smile at us, and sway.
You know that song since six, Jill ... *Yesterday.*

4. Fallout: Five Years Later

Spring Music

(in memory of Egon Dumler)

Philip, Billy, Roger, Bob, and Ted
Won't see this spring, or any other season.
There's not one pair of eyes among the dead.
Spring's rhythmical and rhymed, devoid of reason.
The birds are trilling bits of Bach and Brahms.
The vines are improvising drafts of psalms.
The seemingly senescent cherry trees
Open fresh flowers, pink and white and red
For our gardener listening, eyes closed, on his knees
As if they're whole notes rising from the dead.
The sky insists it's innocently blue,
That nothing happened, Egon, not to you.

The Pond

Nature is never wrong, the lilies say,
Simply alive in the pond, life goes on.
Despite carnivorous violence, firestorms,
We are porcelain quiet. Sit on this bench,
Listen to The Baroque Ensemble play
Music composed during The French
Revolution; cherish the bees
Closed in our petals, close your eyes,
Close them, close yourself in these harmonies.
All civilizations die.

Jeu D'esprit

I wrote a lyric that you said was pure,
Full of voiceless plosives, liquids, sibilants,
And, as a young girl licks an ice cream cone,
You showed me how you rolled it on your tongue
And sweetly said, It's written to be sung
By lovers in the shower as they moan
Or on a carpet in a kissing trance
Or in their twenties making up a tour
Of quiet rooms from Paris down to Vence
Or in their early sixties left alone
As we are, still romantic, in our dance
That's sexy, never clumsy, not mature,
Just loosening young vowels on our tongues,
Which in each other's mouths are always sung

Aging

"After a while we learn to mourn ourselves."

We talked of aging in the dying light,
And large ambitions, small accomplishments,
Of hurtful actions, what we really meant.
We stayed up well into the night.

You said, "We're well for now," though nervously.
"9/11 brought this town disease."
"All valleys of death," I joked, "and leafless trees."
You smiled at me dolorously.

Downstairs our precious block was being lit
For Christmas, strings of lights on all the trees,
Snow falling bit by bit by bit.
You kneeled at the window, childlike on your knees.

Did you ever think we would come to this,
We who lived from kiss to kiss to kiss?
Did you think our bodies would frighten us
When we were free and wild and dangerous.

As Time Goes By

That was a golden age in which we lived.
Each day was summer, God was everywhere,
In every molecule of New York City air
When we were young and just believed in us.
That was a haloed age in which we lived,
Late twentieth century summer, love was everywhere.
I'd stop beside you on our walks to stare
At you, buying a peach, climbing a bus's stair.
And there were buts, but always and & and
Sitting in Central, doodling each other's hand,
And I recited poems, my simple fictions
In meter, rhyme, and New York City diction.
As dusk drew near we'd hold a darkening kiss.
When you're distressed, you must remember this.

Dusk

After years of tragedies wearing us thin
As butterflies, as delicate and transient,
We find each brownstone brick, each flowerpot
Our eyes alight on, seemingly heavensent.
And each late hour seems a moment to begin,
A perch defining who we were and who we're not,
Beautiful to each other in our darkening shades,
Dark as these interior walls and balustrades
Where ghosts of Whistler, Sargent, Merritt Chase
Unravel a glove with almost living grace,
Walking toward their future in a distant room
Where butterflies are fixed, cut flowers bloom.

Re-reading

When we re-read the fictions of our lives,
The genre changes with the characters
And what, for instance, seemed a bawdy comedy
Becomes, with consequences, tragedy,
And our best qualities become our worst.
So bravery, for instance, and tenacity
Become impulsiveness, rigidity …
Often re-reading is like reading Braille
When we're not blind—we see it makes no sense
Anymore than a sleepwalker's dream,
Our arms outstretched for meaning, till Time wakes us
To what is strangely present, dangerous.
And so in many colors, tongues we pray,
God have mercy on us, God have mercy on us.

Acupuncture and Mozart

Calmed at my heart meridian, I spin
Mozart to pirouette on his royal blue disc.
His strings are dainty and his woodwinds brisk.
His keyboard strokes sound quaintly feminine.

Mozart's metronome, invisible and mute,
Leads me to find my mother with my *chi*
—Unblocked, pure kinesthetic memory
Urged on by oboes, violins, and flutes

—All fingers trilling. Now a bow drawn slow-
Ly across the body of a cello
Quiets the strings to weep *adagio*.
The cello double stops and the winds gasp, Oh!

Now a solo grieving violin
Sings on the E string how it can't take death.
I watch my mother's Quan Yin hold her breath.
It's time again for mourning to begin.

* Quan Yin is the goddess of *chi,* our life force according to
Chinese medicine.

The Frick

Overwhelmed by beauty I weep for life
Now that I'm frail, now that I have been sick.
I stroll past Titians, Bellinis with my wife
Into the great long chambers of the Frick

Where huge Turners and Whistlers are lit
As if their lifetimes still exist. Their ships
Sunsets, gowns, shadows, counterfeit smiles
Bespeak seduction from long vanished lips,

Like Vermeer's Lady's who now makes me weep.
As do Rembrandt's characters in theatrical dress,
Even his Polish Rider now long asleep,
And the model for the soldier by Velazquez.

Life, life in Frick's artificial garden,
Where lovers lounge in well-protected planes.
Here Frick at night would wander, stricken
By his daughter's death; only art could keep him sane.

And so his wealth and generous collection
Were like two pockets filled with gold
Coins he could rattle like recollections
Which in his helpless grasp turned simply old.

Resonance

Three centuries have passed since she peeled fruit,
Dressed in red and brown and linen white,
Her knife glistening, though it's still and mute.
She sits in silence for Nicolaes Maes.

A napkin on her lap folds in the light
Slipped from the wall, as if light stays.
A skein of skin, a cello's backwards "S"
Waits for its twin, though the knife can't turn.

Her hands hold still, as if they've come to rest
Upon a note a cellist's stopped to coax us,
To keep our eyes, like Maes, simply in focus
On what's to come, but what remains unheard.

Afterword

In an essay, "Trauma and Poetry: A Psychoanalyst's View of the Healing Power of the Arts" (*Partisan Review, Spring 2003*), I showed how I came to write the lyric sequence, "The Unholy Dark" and the dramatic monologue "Dark Carnival." Since the sequence and monologue make up part of this book, I thought I would include this brief essay as an *Afterword.*

*

Since the earliest days of Freud and his followers, psychoanalysts and literary critics have tried to construct theories of creativity that link the arts and the art of psychoanalysis, My ideas about the relationship between them come from my work both as a poet/playwright and as a practicing psychoanalyst. They have found their way into my literary criticism and psychoanalytic essays having to do with dramatic structure, meter, rhyme, and particularly metaphor.

In twenty-five years of doing clinical work, I have learned to listen carefully for one key metaphor which, repeated throughout treatment, helps uncover memories of trauma and the unconscious fantasies attached to them. The metaphor in its many permutations comes to structure all of treatment which fascinatingly reflects a split in the psyche that shock and fantasy have created.

By bringing these metaphors over and over again into the psychoanalytic dialogue, I can help my patients heal their splits and revise their life narratives.   That this can happen at all is because the mind has a *natural* propensity to use metaphors and dramatic techniques for internalizing trauma and, if we're lucky, for self-healing after trauma.

We can see how natural this self-healing process is when we look at those dreams in which we psychically revise both private and public trauma. We give ourselves the *nocturnal* distance we need by turning the actual details of trauma into dream metaphors, and by dramatically making other dream characters suffer the trauma with our dream selves safely watching.

In our *waking* life we see the same natural attempts to repair trauma by creating and participating in the arts. During the walling in of the Warsaw Ghetto, for instance, right up until the boxcars were sealed, there were more theatrical and musical performances, art exhibits, and poetry readings than ever before in that city. Creativity has a considerable healing power, more potent and sophisticated than our mere dreams. Creativity gives writer and reader, painter and viewer, composer and audience a safe place to re-experience emotions that have been stunned into silence. It does so partly by making a bridge of metaphors connecting and creating distance between what we knew and felt and what we didn't want to know or feel.

In our own time, right after 9/11, many psychoanalysts such as myself had to try to heal themselves along with their traumatized patients. As I tried to help my patients articulate their past personal and public traumas that were instantaneously connecting to this new one, I simultaneously tried to help myself by writing poetry. I helped ward off post-traumatic stress symptoms from developing by first writing a long lyric sequence, "The Unholy Dark," structured in part by using the key metaphor of *the lost home,* one that I had used in my earlier work.

"The Unholy Dark" helped me metaphorically connect the 9/11 trauma with earlier ones, and to set in motion a mourning process for the lost home that I had been unable to complete before. But even this mourning process would turn out to be only partial until months later when I dramatized the aftermath of the disaster in *Dark Carnival: A Dramatic Monologue.*

My wife and I were home when the first plane hit. My son who lived downtown saw it and called us. We turned on the t.v. and watched transfixed as action movie fantasy turned into reality. That day, and through the rest of the week as I listened to my patients, I found that the towers quickly became metaphors for parents who had died, or had crumbled for them in childhood or adolescence. These metaphors showed up in their dreams and just below the surface of their daylit dialogue. At the same time, I saw how the fall of the towers were also connected for *me* with the death of my parents, and the clustered deaths of my extended family.

Just months after my son was born, my father died from a flu shot—an ordinary American object, like a commercial jet. Afterwards my second tower, my mother crumbled emotionally, and then died of a heart attack.

As I was beginning to write "The Unholy Dark," I found I was connecting the rescue efforts at 9/11 to my failed efforts to rescue them. (I had warned my father not to take that shot, and tried to stop my mother's long fall.)

Further back, the disaster and rescue efforts connected to my being three years old and watching my mother fall down unconscious, seemingly dead.

It also hooked into another public disaster I was directly involved in—trying to rescue children during the Nigerian Civil War. Then, in my twenties, I realized I was also trying to rescue my mother's childhood from the pogroms she had witnessed in Russia. Here is the first poem I wrote in "The Unholy Dark":

In the Restaurant

I'm served by Erica, badly exposed
To Chernobyl burning in those breakfast years,
Scrambling her cells to terrorist cells
Just miles from where my mother witnessed Hell.
"By smell," she says, "we're forced to witness this
Crematorium mixing bone and skin,
Spreading up here like metastasis ...
And your son watched the two planes hit, and your
Brother-in-law escaped from a top floor?
So eat," she smiles like Mom, "You're getting thin."
And time and place collapse and the dust blows in.

*

As the days following 9/11 limped on, I realized the poems I was writing were developing into a sequence connecting the present disaster with still earlier public and private traumas. I might say that preconsciously as well as consciously, I was making bridges symbolically between this event and the fantasies it generated with split-off earlier ones whose full meaning and emotional impact were becoming clearer to me as I wrote. From my own neuropsychoanalytic point of view, I might say that I was storing as metaphors and symbols my experience of 9/11 in my brain's cortico-limbic system, with the aid of the self-hypnotic effects of meter and rhyme to prevent long-term kindling of neurons that result in Post Traumatic Stress Syndrome. Or, to put it yet another way, in the unconscious time doesn't exist, and by using metaphors, meter, and rhyme, I was trying to place the experience of this trauma and loss in the larger, more time-bound narrative of the poetic sequence, thereby revising my life narrative as I had told it in earlier poems.

One of the recurring themes of the new sequence and of my earlier poems is the relationship between the loss of my childhood home and my bucolic home in the Berkshires. For instance in 1994, I had written

The House We Had to Sell

This is the house we lived in, white as a bride.
Mozart is echoing the birds outside.
We're sitting at the table playing gin.
My son is laughing every time he wins
Because he's eight, because we're all in love,
Living the future we're still dreaming of.
Spring is in the mountains, green as Oz,
In the fresh-cut flowers in the crystal vase,
Mirroring the garden where the bees are thick.
Though everyone was dying, dead or sick,
These were our uncontaminated hours,
Like bottled water sipped by scissored flowers,
Permanent in memory, sealed by the pain
That childhood ends, and we can't go home again.

*

Here, under the impact of 9/11, I looked for that home again, now through the eyes of my grown son:

On the Cell Phone

You're in the Berkshires with your girlfriend—"Hi!"—
And, though our house has long been ruined and sold,
You're driving past it where our road is still
Turning, as always, burning red and gold,

And we're still in Manhattan, me and Mom,
Our Towers ancient rubble, smoking still,
And only seven years have passed, and we
Are drinking scotch to kill the coming chill.

And now that our retreat is gone (we knew
When we first bought it, it would come to this),
I'm singing *Heroism's* final song
About how lovers live from kiss to kiss

Until their autumn ends in killing snow
Falling on rooftops, boxcars, empty streets,
And you are bumping on our narrow road
And blowing kisses at our last retreat,

And in those windows, as in memory,
We're cooking, reading comics, writing poems
About this future that we knew would come,
Though we were safely sitting still at home.

*

Finally, the theme of my lost childhood home and my lost home in the Berkshires came together in "Half the Office," which describes half my psychoanalytic office. In it are both a painting of a house reminiscent of our house in the Berkshires and a Chinese vase from my mother's house. In this process of self-healing, the poem moves the theme and key metaphor of mourning *the lost home* into one of re-attachment and reconciliation:

Half the Office

What seemed unnoticed when the towers fell
Now seems symbolic, lasting, luminous,
As if disaster cast a magic spell
On the merely simple, merely beauteous.

A print of Dürer's St. Jerome, a gift
Our oldest friends brought back from Amsterdam.
The meaning of his contemplation shifts
Now that they're ill. His forehead seems a lamp

By which I see our youthful lust and zest
After our dinner, after the end of light.
His eyes are dim, he needs a little rest.
And so we lie back down and say goodnight.

Next my diploma, 1984,
For psychoanalytic training, and
A store-bought painting of a farm house door,
Blue like our Dutch Colonial, and land

With its luscious fruit trees—apple, peach, and plum,
Its grape arbor with its ancient moss-stained swing,
Its violet beds and staked delphiniums,
Its bluebirds, and its bluejays bickering.

Below the door, irises in profusion,
Stuffed in a basket colored copper, tin.
We bought our house in Time for its seclusion.
Our road once faced the Berkshires' oldest inn

Where then only haystacks stood, their lights the stars
Our son would reach on tiptoe, trying to snatch
Fireflies, one hand Venus, one hand Mars.
It vanished as if Time blew out a match.

What is the meaning in this Chinese vase
Mom left, four scenes of mother and child
In daily tasks made fabulous as Oz?
The child is earnest, Mom is gracious, mild.

For me the meaning's green and porcelain white
And red and green and black with flecks of gold,
And I am seven captive to delight
Though I am nearly sixty-two years old

And I can't mourn her, though I mourned the rest
Who died in clumps like those who disappeared,
And when she fell down dead I got depressed
And lost myself in clouds of childhood fears.

The vase is calm in motion, glazed like hope
Covers me blindly with these simple themes,
Mother and child who will not have to cope

With what's beyond the realm of quiet dreams.

*

For months after finishing what turned out to be a twenty-page sequence, I was uneasy, knowing that I would have to go beyond the narratives of my own life history and dramatize 9/11's impact on my beloved city.

After a few months I realized that what I had to do was to return to the city I had described in *Manhattan Carnival* and write its sequel.

Thirty years before I had celebrated Manhattan exuberantly in the dramatic monologue *Manhattan Carnival*. It is both a book-length poem and play in which the monologist Mark Stern wakes up after an awful one-night stand to search for his estranged wife Marlene:

from *Manhattan Carnival*

"Get up!" Marlene?" I smell the April rain
And squint half-dreaming at the windowpane
Where winter light intensifies to Spring.
I pull the plug so our alarm won't ring,
Then prop myself up on our double bed
And dip to kiss the imprint of your head
And rub your pillow for Aladdin's lamp.
Oh, I'm a sheltered child away in camp!
Get up, she's gone. "Marriage is for the birds."
But who expresses feelings in *those* words?
Stockings, torn underpants litter the floor.
And who's that leering from our bedroom door?

*

Now thirty years later with the city darkened by 9/11, I decided to set Mark Stern on a parallel but much darker journey through more or less the same locations. So now in the Fall of 2002, Mark Stern again wakes up, this time to find both Marlene and their daughter missing, his beloved son-in-law Jack gone for good.

from *Dark Carnival*

"Get up, Mark Stern, it's summer, spring, it's fall,
And winter's coming fast; the caterwaul-
Ing geese, heading for Miami Beach
Fly in a V, perfectly out of reach,
As Jack, twirling bacon on a fork,
Called on his cell phone—then flew from New York
Over New Jersey, south to God knows where,
A soul in freedom, once a millionaire
Broker with Morgan Stanley, handsome Jack,
Sensitive Jack. Mourning won't bring him back.

*

To give me and the reader some more distance from the unfolding tragedy, I tried to summon not only courage but the sense of humor, albeit a darker one, than I had used in *Manhattan Carnival*.

from Manhattan Carnival

I need the window of the Tourist Boards
Of Fifth—their beaches, lower Alps, and fiords –
The students playing clarinet duets,

The mime in top silk hat and epaulettes,
The Hari Krishnas spreading incense, joy,
Their flowing peach robes, shoes of corduroy,
The blind man singing hymns, St. Thomas Church,
The scaffolding where whistling workmen perch,
The haughty English manager of Cook's,
St. Patrick's nave, Rizzoli's picture books,
Tiffany's clock, the pools of Steuben glass,
The pocket park with cobblestones for grass.
Remember how we'd stroll on your lunch hour?
My nickname for you then was "City Flower."

*

from *Dark Carnival*

This Times Square is a souk, a carnival
Where tattooed druggies mix with biblical
Preachers and peep-show businessmen who lurk
For quick fixes before their pin-striped work,
Among the hawkers of fake jewelry,
Americans Al Immortality
Makes prey—Mozambiques and Vietnamese
And Pakistanis, Malis, Japanese
—All splendid decking out the goods we'd sell,
All multicolored, every infidel,
And Saudis, Yemenis, and Sudanese.
America's packed in a valise
Each opens, not a dirty bomb, a vial
Of smallpox—there's no murder in the smile
Of missing teeth or, if they're lucky, gold.
They're all New Yorkers, flashy, chatty, bold
Beneath huge billboards selling underwear

Of gorgeous nudes, huge sculpture in mid-air,
And ads for scotch and DVD's and slacks.
This is what Al Immortality attacks.
The whole square trumpets, *This Is Liberty,*
"These teeming masses yearning to be free"
Of amputation, clitorectomy;
For what these peddlers joyfully declare
Is real Americana: *buy, compare,*
Manhattan Music, passionately rare.

*

Finding some of the courage and sense of humor *I* was searching for helped me repair myself and complete the mourning for my parents, my collapsed towers I had only partially completed in "The Unholy Ground."

As Mark Stern got closer to the unholy ground of the World Trade Center site, I *also* began to understand, self-analytically, what I was doing with the *style* of what I was writing. As in *Manhattan Carnival,* I had deliberately chosen rhyming couplets to echo stylistically the theme of re-unification. Here the same theme repeated itself with Mark, his wife, daughter, and late son-in-law; and also with a city that was trying to come together in defying death. I also had made many passages and lines in *Dark Carnival* parallel those in *Manhattan Carnival.*

But though I knew these conscious reasons for the rhymes, I couldn't understand why I had chosen those nursery rhyme names—Jack and Jill—for my characters. Consciously I had chosen Jack for my missing hero because the name referred us back to an earlier public trauma, to our loss of "handsome Jack/ sensitive Jack" Kennedy, to a similar shock to our innocence when he was assassinated.

But I began to wonder what was involved with my nursery in my original home that made me use Jack *and* Jill? What earlier private trauma was I trying to remember and repair?

When I brought Mark to the disaster site, reuniting him with his family, I suddenly realized I had reversed the generations to reunite my own Jack and Jill in my quest to mourn them: Jack, like my father, brought down by the deadly needle of a plane, and Jill collapsing into despair like my mother: "Jack and Jill went up a hill/ To fetch a pail of water/ Jack fell down and broke his crown/ And Jill came tumbling after."

But it wasn't until a happy coincidence a few months later that I would discover an *unconscious* connection to a very early trauma that most likely had led me to choose not only the names of these nursery rhyme characters, but also the meter of the poem.

A psychoanalytic peer group I had joined was discussing infant research, and a couple of people expressed the conviction that infants really couldn't conceptualize their feelings until two years old. Their comments made me feel oddly trapped and angry. Then I had a flashback to being well under two years old. I saw myself lying on my parents' bed with a bout of severe recurrent ear abscesses, waiting for the doctor to come and puncture them.

I vividly remembered tapping out varying patterns of ten beats with my fingers to distract myself from the pain.

Was this, I thought, the basis for the iambic pentameter in my work, and specifically for the meter in *Dark Carnival* with its many varying feet and caesuras? Certainly the nursery rhyme names, Jack and Jill, at a deeper level, had their origin here. Finally, it seemed that those two jets hitting were not only also metaphorically connected to my father's flu shot   but the terror of the doctor's needles hitting my ears—metaphor originating in the body.

After the meeting I told myself that if metaphor and dramatization   could be derivatives of early traumas and fantasy , then maybe too were   meter and rhyme. Perhaps at its deepest level my own attraction to rhyme, as well as meter, originated in this very early attempt to hold myself together in infancy as I was doing now. And, as I went on with this bit of self-analysis, perhaps too the rescue fantasy driving both the lyric sequence and the dramatic monologue derived at its earliest from a profound wish to have my parents rescue me from both my pain and anger—my anger at them while they held my arms down so the doctor with his needles, like those planes, could pierce.

So in a parallel passage to *Manhattan Carnival's* ending where Mark and Marlene are reunited, *Dark Carnival* ends with a very different reconciliation, one of child and parents that helped me cope with the traumas I've described and helped me heal.

   from *Manhattan Carnival*

   The crowd ignores the dwarf peddling *The News*
   Of murders, bombings, chaos, doomsday. Time.
   We're innocent, let's dance. The only crime
   Is coyness, lady. Let the sun collapse
   And night come, we must shoot our craps
   Once more, must challenge Death to play.
   The jukebox blinks. The song is *Yesterday*.
   A traffic helicopter overhead
   Reports that you're refusing to be led
   Even in celebration, reports the crowd

Is laughing at us arguing out loud
That you should lead, that I think in clichés,
That somehow love remains when love decays,
Reports a man is falling to one knee
And shouting, "Marlene, please re-marry me!"
Reports that you are crying "Yes No Yes,"
Reports that I'm unzippering your dress
And leading you to bed, that you're without
Your diaphragm. "Let's have it now," I shout,
That you shout back, we're coupling like rhyme,
Reports that we're oblivious to time.
I'm coming—do you hear that baby crying
Across the garden where the wash is drying?

*

from *Dark Carnival*

"I've come to mourn him here and, as we've prayed,
We've heard rock music classically played.
I see Jack dancing in a masquerade
With Lady Death—black dress, black hat, white plume
Uptown, crosstown, and in our living room.
He bends her low. She tries to kiss his lips.
He keeps her distant in a graceful dip.
The music swells, and they are out of sight.
I call him, 'Jack, come back to say Goodnight.'
This song is from your time, a haunting melody,
My ghost, '*My darling, save the last dance for me.*'"
Now Jill sits, small, beside me on a stair.
I see Jack dancing, molecules of air
Under the Winter Garden's mosque-like dome
Now cleared of rubble … "Daddy take me home

113

By cab, let's see our skyline as we drive,
As it still stood when Jack was still alive:
The Chrysler Building and The Empire State.
We ate this island whole on our first date
From the Brooklyn Bridge to the George Washington.
Please help me get up with the setting sun
Smearing our skyline with a blinding sheen."
  Come on, let's take our baby home, Marlene.
Let's flag a cab or gypsy limousine.
Let's take her home to thirty years and back
Before another terrorist attack
(Their bodies shaved, their eyes all deadened black)
Attempts to make our skyline disappear.
Let's seize the day, this night, this year.
Let's seize Thanksgiving, Christmas ... Do you hear
That segue, bows drawn slowly as they play.
They innocently smile at us, and sway.
You know that song since six, Jill ... *Yesterday.*

*

To sum up, then: Working with metaphor, plot, characters, meter and rhyme both in the lyric sequence and the dramatic monologue helped me to prevent what might have become psychic numbing, or at best the formation of symptoms. It also helped me stay not only emotionally alive but self-analytical as I listened to my patients talk about what 9/11 and its aftermath meant to them. In writing poetry between and after sessions, I was not only better able to help them but, moving *dramatically* to reconciliation at Ground Zero, to heal myself as well.

LaVergne, TN USA
26 August 2009
156056LV00009B/185/P